HALLOWEEN

Harry Behn

HALLOWEEN

ILLUSTRATED BY Greg Couch

A CHESHIRE STUDIO BOOK

North-South Books

NEW YORK · LONDON

Tonight is the night
when dead leaves fly

like witches on switches

across the sky,

when elf
and sprite
flit through
the night

on
a moony
sheen.

Tonight is the night
  when leaves make a sound

like a gnome in his home

under the ground,

when spooks and trolls
creep out of holes
mossy and green.

Tonight is the night

when pumpkins stare

through sheaves

and leaves

everywhere,

when ghoul

and ghost

and
goblin
host

dance
round their
queen.

It's Halloween!

Text copyright © 1949 by Harry Behn. Renewed in 1977 by Alice L. Behn.
Illustrations copyright © 2003 by Greg Couch.
A CHESHIRE STUDIO BOOK
Published in the United States by North-South Books Inc., New York.
Published in Great Britain, Canada, Australia, and New Zealand by North-South Books,
an imprint of Nord-Süd Verlag AG, Gossau Zürich, Switzerland.
Library of Congress Cataloging-in-Publication Data is available.
A CIP catalogue record for this book is available from The British Library.
ISBN 0-7358-1609-3 (trade edition)
1 3 5 7 9 HC 10 8 6 4 2
ISBN 0-7358-1766-9 (library edition)
1 3 5 7 9 LE 10 8 6 4 2
Printed in Hong Kong